Chris Hemingway

paperfolders

Indigo Dreams Publishing

First Edition: paperfolders
First published in Great Britain in 2021 by:
Indigo Dreams Publishing
24, Forest Houses
Cookworthy Moor
Halwill
Beaworthy
Devon
EX21 5UU

www.indigodreams.co.uk

Chris Hemingway has asserted his right under the Copyright, Designs and Patents Act 1988 to be identified as the author of this work.
© Chris Hemingway 2021

ISBN 978-1-912876-53-2

British Library Cataloguing in Publication Data. A CIP record for this book can be obtained from the British Library.

This book is sold subject to the condition that it shall not, by way of trade or otherwise, be lent, re-sold, hired out, or otherwise circulated without the author's and publisher's prior consent in any form of binding or cover other than that in which it is published and without a similar condition including this condition being imposed on the subsequent purchaser.

Designed and typeset in Palatino Linotype by Indigo Dreams.
Cover design by Jane Burn
Printed and bound in Great Britain by 4edge Ltd.

Papers used by Indigo Dreams are recyclable products made from wood grown in sustainable forests following the guidance of the Forest Stewardship Council.

Dedicated to Fern, my daughter.

CONTENTS

Satellite Towns 5
Skype Family Robinson 6
Foxes in Fog 7
Nightwalk (Moped Emptiness) 8
Swans 9
Currency 10
After the Fountain Was Taken from the Mall 11
Skins vs Shirts 12
One Hundred Mayors 13
In Our Province 14
Gallery 15
Hush 16
Cartoon Violence 17
How to 18
On a Lake of Salt 19
Another L-shaped Room 20
When the Poet 21
Resting a Calligraphy Brush 22
Letter to Shareholders 1st April, 2051 23
When the Traveller Knows that he's Closer to Home 24

Satellite Towns

Let's send drones
to the satellite towns,
but not like that Betjeman poem.
Ship household essentials
to pale residentials,
shoppers who never leave home.

Let's despatch dreams
to the dormitory towns,
to fend off their fear of the dawn.
Mitigate losses
for mythical bosses,
leaders who never leave home.

Let's click and let's swipe
in the bachelor towns,
from a short-let luxury lounge.

To another Skype marriage
in the WiFi carriage,
a husband who never comes home.

Then the sunspot struck.
The lines went dead.
"Stock up, lock down"
came the call.
But no-one knew how,
or wanted to anyway.
animal arcs,
crossing the motorway.

We orbit the towns, faces to faces.
Like primary contacts
with alien races.

Skype Family Robinson

We are not a science fiction family.
We are children of traffic jams,
spam salads and Instant Whip.
We keep cupboards in cupboards
under the stairs.

Yet here we are jumping platforms,
photographing passwords
in community espionage.

We are not a desert island family.
We are route maps jotted on plain postcards,
Radio Times, cut-out-and-keep.
We store stamp hinges in tobacco tins
for rainy days like these.

Yet here we are learning languages
at fingertip touches of virtual buttons,
scrolls on tiny dictionaries.

We are not pioneer spirits.
We are 'Softly, Softly'
'Dad's Army' and 'The Beiderbecke Tapes'.
We share rooms, but not eye contact,
with large evasive mammals.

Yet here we are spacewalking,
making light
of all these gravity pills.

Foxes in Fog

At first she thought they were dogs
brushing his heels,
domestic shapes in the thickening fog .

But then five, seven, eleven,
tawnier, redder, crossing the car park.
A duskworld.

He gathers scraps from the folds of his coat.
Conjures swirls from these foxes.
Carnival blizzards, that could turn to snow.

He will not tame them,
he doesn't want to.
He wants to be ringmaster, for this night only.
He doesn't see her.
He thinks he's alone.

Nightwalk (Moped Emptiness)

The Honda C90 is not an iconic machine
at the best of times.
And when the engine splutters out
at midnight,
it is not the best of times.

For reasons of personal safety
this has to be a pavement trip.
To wheel it back to Manchester
before dawn.

Skirting Altrincham,
it's 1985,
streetlights are low priority.
Past Manchester Airport,
automorphic grounded planes
give Disneyesque smiles of encouragement.

In Wythenshawe,
telepathic youths flicker in the shadows,
assessing the scrap value of man and machine.

"Smiths fan, leave him, he's not worth it,"
they mutter.

I pass a sign welcoming me to Gatley,
my 12th suburb.
This could have been
the world's most downbeat calendar.

Now I'm home, and it's 6 a.m.
An hour later, I set off for work,
relieved (for once)
that there's no water cooler,
and very few moments.

(Title taken from *Motorcycle Emptiness* by Manic Street Preachers)

Swans

Where is the silence?
Where are the words?
Where are the gliders?
Where are the birds?
Are we jumping the train?
Or tied to the track?
All the wings of the world
can't carry us back.

Tricked by ambition,
persuaded to run.
And stand in the storm,
or walk in the sun.
In deep meditation,
a paperplay.
In Tokyo neon,
blow them away.

Where was the purpose?
Where was the rhyme?
Where are the moments?
Where is the time?

Currency

In the now, we are balanced.
The coin is round,
ensuring ends meet.

In the moment,
gold is standard.
The mayor paves the streets,
as a precaution.

In the now,
we are more content to be bankrupt.
When our grossest national products
are instruments of torture.

In the moment
cash is a cipher for anxiety,
and algorithms are calculated illusions.
In the now,
we would settle for less.

After the Fountain Was Taken from the Mall

Like lipstick traces
sketched in rust.
Now the wishing coins are gone.

Like tea leaves stretched
across a riverbed.
Has your future diminished?
Now the wishing coins are gone.

Bronze and silver
crossed the palms.
Now the coins are gone,
they'll just dig deeper.

Blasts rock secret caverns.
Stripping wishes
from buried lamps.

Skins vs Shirts

When PE as a whole is some shade of hell,
with seven rings of awkwardness
(like an embarrassed Olympics,
with two extra continents).
Then the basketball practice,
and the casual suggestion,
of skins vs shirts,
is the cheek-burning fiery core.

Mr James leads by example,
and we all wish he wouldn't.
And even as shirts
(which are really just vests),
scars from TB jabs still topping our shoulders.
This basketball practice,
is a gym full of rabbits
in body image headlights.

Mr James perspires heroically,
and we all wish he didn't.
But the skins will never win.
And even the shirts,
who are really just vests,
will never compete
with the jackets.

The jackets, who,
at ease with themselves
calmly stroll around the court,
"Play up!" they call,
striding past Mr James,
the skins and the shirts,
and the hoops they've never needed
to jump through.

One Hundred Mayors

Each Spring
we place one hundred mayors around the city.
Blank canvasses to project upon.

Feral nightshades, surrealistic illusions,
bring to life the lions and hares,
but frighten when they're worn by mayors.

One is covered in mosaic mirrors
to better reflect local surroundings.
Pigeons seeking restrooms lobby unsubtly.
Bodyshape curves distort our viewpoints.

At the end of each summer,
sold off to the highest bidder,
they appear at parties, like static clowns.
Stand around uselessly,
in lobbies of foreign offices.

Neighbours shake their heads,
but this is what we are now.
The city of the fibreglass mayors.

In Our Province
(from the painting: *Fuchun River* by Song Wen Zhi)

In our province
the forests are drenched with ink.

We pipe it to the town.
Fill our quills and palettes
as if we are bottling the night.

The river seems bleached by comparison.
Boats, almost transparent,
drift through our inkworld,
garnishing with sombre songs.

It was hard at first,
but we have learnt not to leave
blots on the horizon.

Gallery
(from the painting *Ennui* by Walter Sickert)

In the guest house,
he stubs cigar ash into a muddy glass,
drags his red-rimmed eyes
towards the window,
lets it slur the street outside.

In the corner,
tired of her reflection,
she finds a moments sleep.

The bell jar makes her think of Beauty,
and another courteous Beast.

But tobacco stains
render the walls
still, undreamt.

He hung her portrait
to hide the markings there.
May 23rd 1919,
the day the room caught fire.

Hush
(from the painting *Sound* by Rembrandt)

Follow my hand,
my silencing hand.
These pages could scatter on the wind.
These words could grow quiet,
but I will not point a finger,

raised, as if manicured.
Look hard enough,
and you can see your fortunes
flicker on the fingernails
of my silencing hand.

Cartoon Violence

Lines drawn,
overlaid, repeated.
Flick through pages
till the pictures blur.
Hide the mirror.
Walk away.

Add a soundtrack.
Could just be whispers.
Adjusted later, corrected.
Close your eyes.
Walk away.

Moulding clay,
a blemish shows.
Curled into a ball.
Take a picture,
then another.
Walk away.

How to

With words, or a lack of words.
With smiles, or an absence of smiles.
Coming home later,
staying up longer.
With excuses, or no more excuses.

In haste, or with hesitations.
In motion, or lost to stillness.
Losing memory,
losing positions.
In time, or without time.

With regret, or with dismissal.
With remorse, or a beginning of remorse.
The day is over,
the night is over.
With one bound, with one bound.

On a Lake of Salt
(from the woodblock *Two Women on the Lake at Enoshima* by Utagawa Kuniyoshi)

So you found me on a lake of salt.
Where clouds like deep blue dragons
roar at the mountain.
Which splits and curls, from sky to floor,
smoke, river, serpent.

It's how I tilt my head.
The salt-trek leaves me tired,
unwilling to flinch any further
to your authority.

I'm sitting on the ice, or is it salt?
Finger poised, in elegant debate.
Shout all you like,
no one can hear above that dragon wind,
the cracking at the mountain's end.

Another L-shaped Room

Tomorrow she'll leave these walls behind,
with their smell of Woodbines and magnolia,
which never fades or dries,
and step into another L-shaped room.

Where bottles, jars and magazines
can stay half-opened.
Where the shelves will creak,
and speak in tongues
of vivid art animals.

Where the cover to the visitors book
can be quietly removed,
as from tomorrow
it will be a diary.

When the Poet

When the poet
no longer sees the moon.
When no stars shine
or night beasts call
in metaphor.

When their words
are just fragments of recurring dreams.
Tiring and tired
in conversation,
of conversation.

How to respond?
Tell them to write what they know.
And if in the moment they know
only sparse skies and silence,
then tell them to write about that.

Resting a Calligraphy Brush
(from a calligraphy brush rest on display at the Oxford Ashmolean Museum)

In a pause between words,
at a station of ideas.
A melting pot,
or the appearance of one.

The brush is rested.
To let him draw
(at the very least) inspiration.

In a time without words,
even then,
these markings could pause us
in our darkbound tracks.

Lit by faces,
gathering on bridges.
Stepping away
from the glowering mountain stumps.

Letter to Shareholders 1st April, 2051

Dear shareholders,
It is with regret, that I have to inform you that today our last broadband network closed down. I feel we are bowing to the inevitable, now the Leader has decreed that poetry is the required mode of communication in our market segment.

Our business model needs to change, but there are positives. Security costs will be lower, as tabloid journalists will find messages more difficult to interpret. We are also able to abandon our plain English policy, as surrealism and metaphor are now acceptable business practice.

We are moving from charging for minutes or megabytes, to a cost per syllable. We will offer discounts for haiku.

Wage bills will be lower, as poet becomes the dominant profession. Many poets would be visibly disturbed at the prospect of earning even a moderate salary.

Quills will be ubiquitous. We will offer pigeon feathers to all customers, and to the contracted, increasingly gaudy plumes, from genetically modified birds of paradise.

When the Traveller Knows that he's Closer to Home
(from the woodblock *Fujikawa* by Utagawa Hiroshige)

When the snow fills the trees
into swollen white silhouettes.
When the summit can show him
every layer of sky.
When he watches each rooftop
and their perfect curve.
When friends can gather
on the new fallen ground.

When his panniers are empty from the journey.
So his horse's hooves keep the ice at bay.
So the journey may finish before nightfall.

Acknowledgements

With thanks to the editors of the following magazines and poetry sites, who have taken versions of some of these poems: *Sarasvati, Picaroon Poetry, Atrium Poetry, Three Drops From a Cauldron, Riggwelter, iamnotasilentpoet, Dear Reader.*

Thanks to Louise Larchbourne, Lina-girl Mhyana and The Ashmolean Museum Poetry Tours for sources and inspirations for the woodblock poems.

Thank you to Jennie Way, Anna Saunders and Jennie Farley for their support and encouragement in pulling this collection together.

And thank you to Dawn and Ronnie for picking these poems, and for working with me to get them out in print – it's been a pleasure!

Indigo Dreams Publishing Ltd
24, Forest Houses
Cookworthy Moor
Halwill
Beaworthy
Devon
EX21 5UU
www.indigodreams.co.uk